THE WEIGHT OF WAITING

Limiting the negative voices
in your head while passing
through the various
time zones of your life.

Peace Amienghemhen

The Weight of Waiting
Copyright @ 2020 By Peace Amienghemhen
First Publishing June 2020

ISBN: 9798654580344

Published by: **FineLines Publishers**
190 Aba Rd, New GRA 300001,
Port Harcourt, Rivers State, Nigeria

E-mail: info@finelinespublishers.com
Or reach us on the Internet: www.finelinespublishers.com

For further information or permission, address:
FineLines Publishers
E-mail: info@finelinespublishers.com
Or reach us on the Internet: www.finelinespublishers.com

Cover Designed by GIPHICS
Vector Image Designed by: Freepik

DEDICATION

I dedicate this book to every single person waiting at various phases of their lives for that special thing. You possess an incredible amount of strength. My deepest desire is that you reduce the weight on your shoulders by silencing the negative voices in your life.

I see you!

I feel you!!

I love you!!!

ISAAC OYEDEPO

Thank you for constantly showing me how to bring Heaven to Earth through your revival flames. Your level of excellence pushes me to never settle for less.

Thank you for teaching me by example how to embrace my *'YOUniqueness'* in its entirety.

Thank you for always leaving the door of mentorship and fatherhood open.

Amidst your tight schedule, the selfless way you *'father'* is a conscious reminder of how God sees us.

Your passion and drive is contagious. Thanks for constantly using your flames to light my candles!

ACKNOWLEDGEMENT

To Trinity (God- Father, God-son, God-Holy Spirit), you unraveled the layers of weight that most of us carry around while waiting. Thank you for making me a willing pen in your hand. *The Weight of Waiting* wouldn't have been birthed without you Trinity!

To my darling hubby, Ben, thank you for being the wind beneath my sail and for seeing at first glance how much of a blessing this would be to the world. Love you B!

To my son, Nathan. Be rest assured that your energy will never be used to lift these weights. I've gone through them so you never have to. My ceiling, no matter how great, will be your floor. Love you!

To my parents and siblings – You guys are simply incredible. Your constant belief in me pushes me and I'm blessed to have you all in my corner.

To Austin Imoru, thank you for your guidance along this path and for seeing this come to life.

To Emmanuel Afiawari, your level of commitment and dedication is noteworthy. Thank you for proof-reading with your eagle eyes.

To my buddies and friends who have inspired from a close range: Solu Nwaobi, Christian Lasbery, Sarah Jonathan, Hannah Osagiede, Priscilla Emefiene, Ayomikun Dada, Bukola Latinwo, Ayodeji Elijah, Omosigho Ozo, Yinka Nwanjoku, Oyenmwen Obasogie and Oghogho Osayimwen. You guys have been super *Ah-Mazing*!!!

FOREWARD

The Weight of Waiting is an extremely inspiring book that everyone aspiring to discover how to navigate the various seasons of life must read.

Have you ever wondered, 'What in the world is going on?' Have you ever asked yourself, 'What do I do?' Have you ever felt, 'Am I the only one in the world going through this pain?

The questions you have asked in secret can now be answered in this amazing book.

Everyone has to learn to deal with negative voices. Your life is like an ear-in monitor with a mixer. You are the sound engineer. You can choose to reduce or eliminate negative voices. You can also choose to increase positive voices.

Peace Amienghemhen (a.k.a CodyBanks) uses an amazing writing style and reader-engaging approach to pull you into the narrative. Her words are drawn from her personal experience. You will observe that the moment you begin to read.

This is an authentic book.

I have pastored, observed and mentored Peace. She has a lot to say on this subject. She has been able to navigate through the various time zones of her life, limiting the negative voices and now has a voice. Her voice will inspire and encourage you to do the same.

Go beyond what is written. Read with an open heart and you will see the love of your Heavenly Father knitted in the fabrics of each chapter.

It is a short read but has a powerful and relatable content.

Come into a place, a new place of clarity, to help you demystify the mystery of life.

Isaac Oyedepo
Pastor, Winners Chapel International
Maryland, USA

Contents

Introduction

Nature has a way of making wisdom sit in the first class section of our hearts. However, not everyone has the currency required to pay for such wisdom. A kind that cannot be bought with money alone but this kind truly has to be bought with something else that we do not just acquire, instead it's something we activate on our inside with the currency of insight. Most of us are privileged to have two eyes but not all of us have seeing eyes. I strongly believe seeing eyes which I call *'insight'* is when our spiritual eyes, physical eyes and mind's eyes can operate in the same frequency.

The Weight of Waiting gently unravels the subtle but heavy weights you have placed between your ears and hearts that are slowly but surely dragging you into a crawling posture when you really should be soaring.

Take a close look at a camel or a donkey, you'd notice they are mostly used for carrying heavy loads and no matter how fast you want them to move, they are limited. The Cheetah and Deer are fast movers, they travel light! Birds in the sky do not require a motivation to take flight.

If that illustration seems a little too far-fetched, let's examine an aeroplane. There's a reason why you are given a *'luggage limit'*. Some international flights that once allowed two pieces of luggage, have changed that to just one. This shows the importance of travelling light if you want to go far. As you'd notice the farther the journey, the less luggage you are advised to carry.

With an open mind, simply relax as you shed every unnecessary weight on your life's journey. Whether it's the weight of people's opinion, weight of anxiety, weight of anger, weight of exhaustion from singlehood, weight of joblessness or weight of failure.

This book will give you a mind shift that will make you recognize the gifts embedded in the journey as you move towards your destination.

Chapter One

Wait! How did We Get Here?

We are a sum total of who we give our ear-attention.

'Show me your friend and I'd tell you who you are' has

been rephrased to '*Show me your friend and I'd tell you where you're going*'.

I once heard a story of two boys (10years and 14 years) who went skiing, the older boy fell in a ditch in the snow and this happened to just be after experiencing some heavy snowfall in that area. All of a sudden the younger boy thought to himself that before he would call out for help based on their location, there's a possibility that he might lose his friend. So he found a log and used it to pull his friend out. Shortly after, people gathered and asked how the boy was able to rescue him. His friend's response was profound '*my friend was able to do it because there was no one to tell him that he couldn't*'.

Those words happen to be the beginning of most people's confusion and frustration. They allow the words of everyone to cloud their personal convictions.

So, they don't feel good until they hear someone tell them they look good.

They think the job they currently have is the worst ever because they listened to another who has done same job and complained all through so they naturally drift towards seeing their job in a bad light.

They think the beautiful girls they've got are not complete simply because society makes them feel they are worthless without a boy child.

They think they are supposed to overthink each step because they've listened to someone they admire remind them of how risky their own ideas were with examples of how badly it ended for them.

They've heard all manner of tales about how bad of a decision it is when you marry someone who is from another country/tribe or how bad it is when the guy is younger than the lady or how wrong it is when the age difference is too much or too little, so their ultimate search already has a malfunctioning start.

Basically, you get the drift as the list is endless.

But here's the thing, the only way you're feeling this way is because you've refused to filter your ears and heart.

If their compliment gets you that excited, their criticism will crush you. You need to exercise caution on the control you give to others over your self-worth and life in general.

Now that we know how we got here, let's take the next right steps that will get us to our destination.

Chapter Two

Waiting for an Escape from the Pressures of Life

Truth be told, I'm not going to act like it's easy to ignore words that come in-between the gates of our ears and I'm also not going to deny the fact that sometimes it feels like we almost can't help it especially when we are constantly soaked into such an environment or community.

Sometimes the people that surround us are often closely related to us or how can we detach ourselves from the words of our parents, brothers, sisters, boss, colleagues, husband, wife, fiancé or best friend. We think the enemy we're fighting is a total stranger but most times they come wearing very familiar capes. This does not in any way tag your loved ones as an enemy, before you have your religious antennas all up in the air. Rather, it sees words that don't align with your beliefs as the enemy irrespective of how closely knitted you are with the vessel it comes through.

Recently, I had a chat with a friend of mine currently based in Canada, few years ago she relocated from Nigeria to Canada and for her, the decision was simple. It was not just about the economy or stress that probably contributed and solidified her decision but in her words it was mainly because of the 'community'. Immediately she mentioned that word I understood the depth she was speaking from.

"The power you give to those who you lend your ear-time to is so crucial."

So what do you do when you can't relocate per say or detach yourselves from those voices? As with many things in life, there are always many options, usually it depends on the situation at hand or the unique individuals you might be dealing with at that point in time. What works for one person just might not work for another. The option you end up using also depends on your discretion of what is right per time (instincts will come in handy). Depending on each situation, I'd describe what strategies I use both to keep my world in check to avoid losing it to the opinion of others and more importantly I'd share strategies I use to stay fully present in embracing my journey as I look forward to each destination.

Chapter Three

Waiting for Love at the Marriage Bus-stop

Love is such a beautiful thing. True Love makes you feel like you're in heaven while on earth, you could almost find yourself silently telling someone to prick you a little bit just to prove that this beautiful feeling is real and you're not dreaming. While that in itself feels so fly, truth is there's such a burden that comes upon most who are not in any relationship.

If you're at the bus stop of finding love, you may not have been in any relationship at all that progressed positively or if you recently broke up with your partner, I feel you. Deep down it feels like there's this anxiety that comes with the month of February because it's been tagged by society as the month of love and in no time, everyone will start showcasing the glitz and glamour of what it's like to be in love and how crazy in love they are with their loved ones.

With all the updates across social platforms screaming love in your face at every turn (which happens to almost be daily), it could make you stop for a minute to think about your own life. It's in those moments you'd remember your age once again and start to recount the '+' or '-' in comparison with those you rate as your peers who may or may not be married.

While you're locked up in your closet, you really try to be strong about it and fight the feeling with self-love but those triggers often make you stoop down and ask God silently "Answer my prayers Lord". The issue at this point with why you feel this way is because you have a mentality of by this age (which society mostly gives), I think I should have been in a relationship already. I'm going to be 35years this year Lord, look at my friend *'Gbemi'*, she isn't up to my social status and she recently shared her wedding invitation card.

First, you all need to chill!

If you keep seeing the race as a sprint this is what is going to happen: you'd dash off and probably run faster than Usain Bolt only to get to the finish line and ask yourself "was that all I waited for so long to get?" because it definitely will feel boring when you get the achievement (in this case your Mr/Miss perfect) as a medal to be won (in most cases not just for you, but to show your world) without enjoying the process.

On the flip side, when you see every single experience including your 'waiting' period as part of your love story it just makes a whole lot of sense.

The next time your mind tries to remind you about how everyone has it going for them in the love triangle, remind yourself that there are also lots of people who would give anything to remain single because they jumped in so quickly before discovering their so-called spouse wasn't everything you thought they were.

No matter how great you think you are, there's always a place for public opinion. It's important we establish that fact which is why a football player on the field will think he did his best yet he might get criticized for missing a shot and believe it or not, the entire team might even think their failure was as a result of the single shot he missed. No hard feelings at all, it's just called *life*.

The easiest way to toughen your skin and deal with it is to remember where you're standing and where they are. You are on the playing field, you're an active player. There are fans, foes and frenemies. Some of them actually care a lot about you, others are so scared they want to place certain fears upon you. Sometimes they tell you they got married really early at about 23years and the tale just never ends.

I believe every single person is 'YOU-nique' and the earlier you own it, the better you'd become.

Just after my Masters overseas, I was fully single after going through a break up with my ex and returning home to meet family, I could hear some tiny whispers here and there as the months progressed and even when they don't say it directly to you, you could almost feel the questions, fears and worries through their smiles, actions and in almost every gesture. Maybe at this point you might think I'm just being paranoid – maybe yes, maybe not.

Literally, it felt like whenever we were seated in an enclosed place it was as if I needed to get out for some air because their thoughts were penetrating through to me in a way. Their fears were tangible. Their love felt spiced with uncertainties.

Truth is, most times our loved ones really love us but they can't help to question every step you take or don't take. Not because they love you less but because they need your lives to be spelt out according to a *script* they've got in their head. Spoiler Alert!!! They do not and should not write the script of your life.

If you bow to their voices, you would have made them a god over your life.

Our Heavenly Dad (God) is the only one who should hold that pen to write your script or the clay to mold your life. The knowledge of this is where your confidence will spring from.

Interestingly, as I got back into the country while trying to settle in once again, a close family member advised me to start attending a particular church as she said they had so many youthful people there. Well, I tend to understand people's words even if they try to hide their motives (part of the pecks of having a discerning spirit)

This time, the idea was to get me to go and mix up with the youth just so I can at least find someone. That was not a bad idea. If you thought I was going to tag it bad, then you got it all wrong! There is absolutely nothing wrong with trying new places or getting comfortable to meet new friends with a possibility of having a relationship with one of them. But it just wasn't right for me.

It is possible to be given a good idea that is bad for you.

A discovery of your personal identity is where it all should begin from. Let's take a particular nut, like groundnut, it has so many benefits and even the dieticians might tell you its usefulness for the body but for me there's a side effect on my face whenever I take it.

Back to my question: *'is groundnut good for one's health?'* I guess yes. But *'is it good for my body?'*

Absolutely not. Exactly! This is how we should approach life.

The level of your self-awareness determines the level of your life's success. No wonder Socrate's said '*know thyself*'.

Immediately she said that statement, I already knew it wasn't a bad idea but it wasn't the right idea for me. Emphasis on me! There's a point in your life when you've walked with God that you begin to embrace so much rest in places that others experience chaos. This part cannot all be taught in one book, it needs to be experienced.

You've got to get to that point in your life where you can listen to people objectively without being trapped by their words in your mind. Usually, this is learnt over time. Like my mentor Adaora Lumina says '*Time is a great story teller*'.

In a world where everyone wants to rush you into getting into a relationship and getting married, no one talks about the place of friendship. They are so eager to see you change your status. People are beginning to place value on the wrong set of things. It seems to me like the world is going insane on what they place their values on. This is why you need to always see and read between the lines as you train your instinct to discern appropriately.

THE PARENTAL SUBWAY OF YOUR LOVE BUS-STOP AND WHAT TO MAKE OF IT

This part might seem a bit tricky. For those of you with parents who are extremely supportive and see you as a full grown adult not by their words alone but actions, I've got some accolades for you and you really should be grateful. Had a chat with a dear friend of mine whose parents are so loving but seem to be holding on too tightly that it seems like their love should be tagged *'Love Gone Wrong'*. I'd explain why in a bit.

In a world of fast advancement, most people are stagnated not because there's an enemy that has marked them per se but they are surrounded with parents, caretakers or a support system that want to believe their children are adults yet won't give them the breathing space they so desire to live like one.

It is great to have love and support but as a parent even when it might be tough and hard, we need to understand when it's time to trust that the lessons we've taught our kids will stick with them. Just as the Mother Eagle does, If we really want that Eaglet to soar, then we must be willing to let it go. Let it flap those wings for a start. Let it figure out how to get food. The sooner, the better. My friend's frustration was the fact that his parents had said the only reason why he'd move out of his house is if he's moving into his marital home. Well, that's a debate for another day.

As much as it might seem easy to point fingers, if you know me then you'd know I strongly believe that the only person your fingers should ever point at should be the person in the mirror.

Not everything is as it seems, you might have to look a bit closer and ask questions.

For instance, in my friend's case there might have been real reasons why his parents act the way they do but until he steps up to act in a polite and reasonable manner with a blend of boldness and respect, he might have to endure whatever pain he feels for a very long time. However, like I said that's a debate for another day.

I'm not going to state what's right for you or not when it comes to the subject of love, relationship or marriage, beyond what anyone (including those of your parents) thinks, you need to make an informed and conscious decision personally. Those voices only exist in your head because you've allowed them to rent a space there. You've loaned them the land for free, so most times the general public have built a bungalow, mansion or even a palace in your mind-space.

It's important you listen to wise words from loved ones but you need to also understand where they are coming from, sometimes some words of advice are the fruits of fear seeds that has been nurtured and developed roots in their personal lives and right now they're trying to create a branch of their roots in your life. I think in Agricultural science such act is described as *grafting*. There are times you have to stubbornly agree to some words by simply nodding just so people can move on but there are other instances that you need to firmly share your view or take your stand if what they're saying has been echoed way too many times. Your voice needs to be stamped. Just remember time is a great story-teller and one day they'd be glad you stood your ground and followed your heart.

BEING ALONE VS BEING LONELY

These are two sides to every coin including this. While you can be alone and not feel lonely, you can feel lonely even when you're not alone. At this point, I'd repeat the words slowly *'While you can be alone and not feel lonely, you can feel lonely even when you're not alone'*. What seems to be the difference?

INNER PEACE

A couple of years ago I was overwhelmed in a way. On one hand, my 9am – 5pm job which was in some cases 6am - 9pm was really taking its toll on me and when I was home, I just had so much I needed to do both for family and personally. But then something happened. I was super-duper excited that the Easter break was just around the corner and I felt it calling my name in a way. Let's just say I knew I needed a big break from everything.

EVERYTHING

I just needed to breathe. I wanted some *me-time*. Sadly, the insecurity issue in the country(Nigeria) at that time was going crazy with bomb blasts everywhere that at a point while at the office, the whole ground vibrated from an explosion. So yeah, it was that scary. Nonetheless, I told myself I just wanted to chill that weekend. I didn't really want to travel out of town because the holiday was just for a weekend yet I didn't want to spend it at home either.

I was seeking something new, something fresh and certainly something refreshing. So I quickly announced at home that I was going away for the Easter break, the idea was to have a mini-vacation not close enough to have my lovely family creep in on my much needed space but also not so far so my safety would be in check as well.

No doubt, this got them all perturbed as they started asking questions and eventually told me to promise them I'd send all the details once I lodged. This to me was a very fair deal. I packed my bags and zoomed for the Easter holiday.

Vacation checklist: My Gadgets. Cool outfits. Mobile Money. A hotel with a very strong

Wi-Fi connection. Great restaurant-service.

Isn't it funny that these days when you say you're going on a vacation and you tell them you're going alone; most people literally think it's not going to be fun. Once again, what's not fun to one, might be close to heaven for another.

Some think there's more to it than just chilling alone and your thoughts are as good as mine on how wild they can cook things up. However, at a young age I grew some pretty thick skin and perfect sieve that has helped over the years to keep me genuinely on cloud 9 when others make up stories without substance to suite their illusion.

Back to my Easter experience which was awesome by the way. I felt elated to say the least. I understood what God meant when he said one day is like a thousand years and a thousand years is like a day before Him. Funny but so true! In those 3 days, I felt like I got the refreshing of 3 thousand years and on my return, I was recharged, refueled and well rested. If you're reading this (especially if you're single), then you really should try it.

In the middle of my groove, my darling sister also confessed that she wished she could join me too. Hahahaha. (*Just a pointer that you've got to listen to whatever makes you tick, first they may question you but later they will join you*). No don't worry she wasn't invited, I was still in town remember, it's not like I travelled far away.

Although, I was alone in the hotel room but I never felt lonely, not for a second. If you're thinking to yourself, 'is this even possible?', then I suggest you try it once in your lifetime. The feeling was out of this world for me so much that I still talk about that experience till date. That is what it means to enjoy and embrace your journey. There's a popular quote that says "*happy singles go on to make happy marriages*". Basically, it is important to see every stage and phase as worthy of celebrating.

Life is a gift, are you really going to unwrap it with grudges of not having what's beyond your control instead of enjoying every inch of it as it unfolds daily?

If your friends are looking fly with their spouses right now, that's Amazing. Celebrate them. Be happy for them. This is their chapter, yours is coming soon and when yours arrives guess what? The whole focus will be on you! Not because you need the attention but because that's just the way life is.

No one reads a book backwards.

So if their story happens at Chapter 2, good for them. Yours is coming soon and when it does, your world will be waiting eagerly to flip yours open. If you can grasp this illustration, you'd come to embrace the Joy in your Journey. Aha!!! That must have been why you can actually find the word JOY in *JOurneY*.

Chapter Four

Waiting for the Dream Job (when 9 to 5 meets with your 24/7)

If you're one of those waiting for days, months or years on a job. A better job. Your first job. A new job. That's Amazing! But there's just one thing you've got to do at this bus stop. You've got to learn to sharpen your axe! There's this analogy about cutting a tree. So let me ask you right away: If you've got an *Iroko* tree you want to cut down, will you just take the axe you kept 2 years ago in your basement and begin to cut it down or will you spend few minutes sharpening the axe before you even begin?

Wondering what to do while you wait for your next job? Don't just wait it out. Work it out. Let the job meet you busy. Do all you can to sharpen your skills like you would sharpen that axe knowing fully well that your pay will be raised higher and your skills will be appreciated better if only you can sharpen better.

Simply waiting for a job can seem like a waste of time but learning skills, volunteering and improving yourself along the way while working towards getting a job becomes time invested which will yield and profit you in the near future.

Have you ever had to wait for a job? This can really be so tough especially when there are so many things hanging in the balance. It's been said that Life is 10% what happens to you and 90% your response to it. Jack Ma, the founder of Alibaba talks about how many times he got rejected at Harvard and how many times he failed in getting a positive response from all his job interviews.

Les Brown, the world renowned motivational speaker failed so many times as he tried getting a job as a *disc jockey*. Every day he went back to the same place he was the previous day just to ask if they had a vacancy and they'd reply *'we just told you yesterday that there wasn't'* and in his response, he'd say well I don't know if someone got laid off or if anyone had died. He kept going there every single day. That must have been an insane approach. However, on this particular day, the manager got fed up of seeing his face and as he approached him, he told him 4 words *'go get me coffee'*, so he became a coffee man. This gave him an opportunity to observe their disc jockey staff (*I like to think he was informal intern - learning the job without necessarily being offered the position*).

At night, he'd practice his intro lines just in case he ever got a chance to. While the manager took his cup of coffee one day, news came in that the disc jockey staff was ill and didn't make it to work. This was Les Brown's open ticket. Shortly after, he was asked if he could handle it and he jumped without thinking twice, that was how he got the job.

Most people get angry at the bus-stop, they get fed up with life, they are so focused on survival mode that they even forget there's more to it than meets the eyes. If you've boarded a plane before you'd understand that what you see on ground and what you see up there are very different. On ground, you've got a myopic view but above the clouds your view is almost heavenly. This is how you should approach every single thing.

Whenever you look, always try to see beyond your human eyes and listen with your heart.

PUSHING THE WHEEL BARROW OF YOUR STARTUP BUSINESS

There are different kinds of jobs and work. In this era, we have quite a number of startup businesses springing up every now and then but then you notice that for some, starting is easy but sustainability is tough and rough. For others, starting is in their thoughts but the chains around their feet are the *'what-ifs'* buried in their minds. These chains are tighter than the fear of their business failing.

Well, Faith is not the absence of Fear.

"Faith isn't just the absence of fear. Faith is the presence of fear but the assurance of the probability of success rising far above the probability of failure amidst the fears"

Your business is as valid as your breath. If you're saying to yourself that you're trying to wait to have the perfect logo, perfect name, perfect staff and even perfect YOU which is a lifetime of infinity. Save yourself the stress and remember there are two rules to this game:

1. Life is about embracing the Journey as you look forward to the destination.

2. Never forget rule number 1

Most times people are looking for complex things but life has been made so simple so why do you try to complicate things. Sticking to the basics will save you a whole lot of headache. If your business is new and you can't raise capital, who says you've got to launch it in the highbrow areas of town. You can start the business from the comfort of your home and gradually scale it up.

"Think Global, Start Local: Be Glocal"

Chapter Five

Waiting for your mini version (Baby zone)

How soon is too soon to expect a mini version of you or even better, a mega version of you. Either way, how soon is too soon? In this part of the continent and particularly in Nigeria, once you are a graduate it seems like the spotlight is focused more than ever on you. First, they are going to come for how important it is for you to get a job. This even seems to be more important to them than learning a skill that will get you that job you so desire. This is what I call *misplaced priorities*!!! So, even if you get a job that pays you considerably enough to your satisfaction but seems too low for those who feel they've got a voice over your destiny, then it becomes another mega problem.

Shortly after, they will come to probe your relationship status, be prepared as this might come in a subtle form of *"when are you settling down?"* or *"which friend are you seeing now?"*. These questions might be re-arranged in many forms but they surely won't be far from this. Once again, the focus is less on how happy you guys are together or about getting to know who this special friend is. Few will sincerely be interested but the rest will be at the finish line of your courtship or starting line of marriage and obviously cannot wait to get their *Asoebi (uniform dress worn for a ceremony in Nigeria)*. Initially we thought such appearance was just prominent in places like Lagos-Nigeria based on their kind of style but it seems like such attitude has crept into the length, depth and width of the entire nation and interestingly also seems to have experienced some form of global osmosis.

When next you're in the U.S or UK and there's a Nigerian party, be rest assured to plan with the mindset that people will turn-up in grand style just like in Nigeria with the code-name of *'mo gbo, mo ya'* (which can be interpreted as *'an uninvited guest who comes basically for the food')*.

If you deviate from their own version of a perfect wedding, be prepared as eyebrows will be raised and another set of questions will be thrown in the air just like the bride's bouquet. Only that this time around, you have to ensure you catch it and respond with the type of answers they are itching to hear. Often times, it won't be thrown at you directly but you will most definitely get a feel of their hearts through the energy they disperse. Good energy and bad energy have vibes that are not hard to miss.

Peradventure you scale the first and second gate, you'd get to the third gate or didn't they say they are three gates in Heaven again?? Lol. Over here, once you get married the joy goes beyond the roof but it seems like that joy is short-lived because a major part of people that surround you have refused to sip from the cup that says *'minding my business'* but have chosen instead to drink from the one that has *'minding other people's businesses'* written all over it.

Unfortunately, 'energy' whether good or bad is extremely contagious which is why the company you keep is so important and critical. Your joy, love and peace can all be short-lived if you entertain someone who constantly stays sad, gossips about others and makes what you have look like trash because they keep pointing over the fence to show you how beautiful the grass is over there. Reminding you of how much the next family has accomplished so much in such a short time and it seems like you haven't started yet. This in no way removes the fact that there are times when you can be motivated by a person's success story. However, when people criticize you without providing a strategy for you to improve, that's definitely a good example of bad energy that needs to be kept far away from you. So the next time, you hear them compare you to another in a bad manner, kindly and sincerely ask what better ideas they have, if they don't please trash it?

My spiritual father and mentor, Isaac Oyedepo gave a unique illustration on how to filter information especially in this generation. He divided them into Trash and Recycle using the analogy of the bin collectors. *How do you know which information to trash and which should be recycled?*

Any information that breeds fear without telling you what to do about it as a way of eliminating or minimizing such fears should be discarded. On the contrary, anything that boosts your faith should be considered and recycled.

During my visit to Toastmasters' (An organization that operates clubs worldwide for the purpose of promoting communication, leadership and public speaking), I learnt a simple principle they use to provide feedback to speakers. It's called the CRC principle and I use this on a daily basis whenever I've got to give feedback to anyone. C-Commend, R-

Recommend, C-Commend. Always kick-off by commending people, next you can recommend and state what changes you'd like them to effect or what you think they could have done better. Finally, always end the feedback session with a commendation as well. It's a Sandwich principle as I like to call it. It works for kids, adults, colleagues, friends, family etc.

Back to my point about what happens in the third gate of your marital journey. The third gate is the interlude between when you get married and when your babies arrive. That wait can be so daunting not necessarily because of how the couple feels but usually because of how others make them feel. Eventually, the couple gets to hear the worries and thoughts of their close friends/families either directly or otherwise and that surely takes a toll on most.

Some of the loud thoughts and whispers you can hear flying around right about that time will usually sound like this:

'It's been 3 months and we doubt if his wife's pregnant yet or have you heard anything?'

'Oh but they got married a year before my friend who just had a baby girl.'

'Please talk to them I really don't know what they are waiting for?'

It's interesting how these stories creep into the ears of those expecting. But that's not even the main issue here.

Do you know there are some people who really want to be married but really would love to be without kids for some years before having children? Before we all get our brows raised and anatomical lenses cleaned up! It's true and their reasons are legit and best known to them. I have a friend who mentioned that once he is married, the early stage of raising children is one thing that scares him. He said if there was a way the kids could be brought to him when they are about 9years or thereabout that would be ideal for him. I found that hilarious but I also understood where he was speaking from. This in no way makes him a bad person and does not remove the fact that he will be a great father but it also shows the underlining fears he has. This is just one example, the next might shock so many that personally know me.

Right after my husband and I got married, although we had courted and gotten to know each other pretty well, we had never lived together so marriage was almost like a second degree phase of courtship for us. Remember what they say *'marriage is a lifelong institution you never graduate from'*.

Lots of people gave the flawed perspective of their personal marital journey to us especially the bump they encountered within the first 3 months and in their words they kept saying we should prepare for such (*isn't it funny how many people try to think just because they made mistakes, everyone had to follow their script and prepare for the same storms*). They talked about how they got to argue over so many things before they eventually got to adjust and sold the idea (which of course we never bought) that we should expect a bumpy ride at the beginning!

Looks like we got the second side of the coin when we got married and when you're on the side of the world that is really sunny, you cannot relate to what people mean when they say they are shivering in the cold. My point is we bonded really well from the beginning and we still do. We still talk about those weird unsolicited advices we got that just never happened to us. This is a clear picture that you usually experience what you expect and work towards.

Due to my understanding of the projected change of attitude (hormonal changes) that could spring up during the pregnancy phase, I sincerely wanted that initial phase of marriage to be spent on us getting to know each other. Truthfully, we needed that personal bonding time and actually enjoyed it. Then the time came when we were ready to expand our family, it seemed like right about the same time friends and family began to have perceived worries and weights of questions about us and when the baby should be expected. Their worries and unasked questions really sought to know if there was something medically wrong with us.

Right about that time, God blessed us with the perfect gift of our lovely son at the perfect time. What we ensured during that waiting season was to never allow the pressure from everyone create a crack within our bond.

Too many that are in this phase, waiting for their own babies who feel their perfect time has passed, always remember that when God shows up, He loves to show off. You'd be the only one the world will be celebrating at that point in time, though the wait might seem long please hang in there.

On the brighter side, if you're in this phase just be grateful that you're even married. It's tough but don't compare yourself with anyone. Don't put your life on hold, keep believing and you will hold those precious gifts in no time.

I believe deeply that the only one that gives human gifts wrapped in baby-like form is God and His timing is impeccable.

Always find a way to stay positive when the whole world keeps reminding you of how unfortunate they think you are. Get back to moments that inspired you the most, Live your dreams - guess what! Some haven't even discovered theirs yet. So if you have, live it to the fullest. Be a beacon of light and hope in the ways you can. Keep blessing lives and the bread you're casting upon many waters will bless you tomorrow as you will reap the harvest of the seeds you're sowing today.

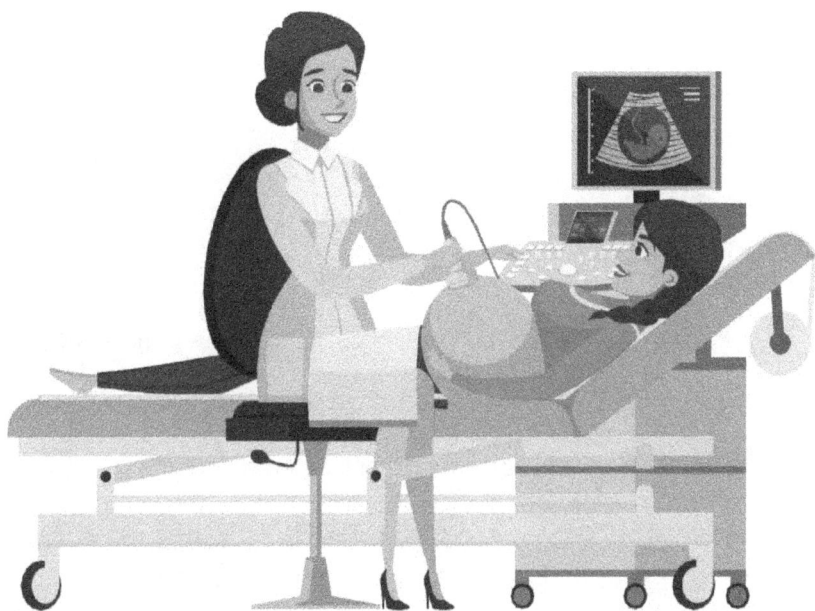

Chapter Six

Waiting for the Baby's Gender Reveal

Just across my sister's house, they had a neighbor who more than anything wanted a girl child. They had the first and second as boys and then they went unto the third who was a boy and tried for the fourth who was also a boy. I just might be wrong but somewhere deep down inside I felt like she was looking for a girl. Maybe the feeling was mutual with she and her husband or maybe she needed it more. Like I said, I just might be wrong. In a world where everyone wants to believe their assumptions are extremely accurate, I love to make room for possibilities that I just might be wrong and very wrong at that and I'm open-minded enough to see things differently.

Fast forward to 4years later, I went to the salon to get my hair done and there was this little girl right there, trying to get some skills up her sleeves. Hmmm, she was just 10years old and I could tell that she was passionate about learning some salon skills. So as the stylist finished getting my hair whipped and was ready to close her shop as she had to dash off, the girl was bored and still stayed around the shop. It was then that we got into a conversation.

I loved the fact that her parents rather than allow her entertain herself with all sorts of cartoons, allowed her to learn a new skill and encouraged her passions. She told me of how she attended various church skilled workshops and in most of the workshops she enrolled in of which she had a passion for, she happened to be the only child there but then I asked if her parents were comfortable with that? She said yes. I asked about her siblings and she said she was the first born with 3 sisters. 2 of which were playing in the compound and the last was just a baby. But without even asking further, she felt comfortable in saying that her mum has desperately been looking for a boy. Now, that part hit me. Why you may ask? Well, it's one thing to so desire any gender, it's another thing for a girl that little to tell me how desperate her mum desired to have a boy. Like, this really hit me!

So I asked, 'why would you even think your mum wants a boy badly' and then she says 'it's because she says it all the time'. There's this evangelist that was always coming to the house to pray probably around the time she got pregnant but he was always in their house praying for a boy. So I could just imagine the disappointment when the child came forth as a girl. Now, my focus and pain was first about the weight this girl carried. She poured it all out like it was a yoke she carried as well. Knowing fully well that children are smarter than we think they are especially in this generation. I really think they should be given more credit than usual.

If you happen to be a Mom in those shoes, while there's absolutely nothing wrong with having sincere desires, preference and needs, it's best to pay attention to the type of vibes you send out. Because even though your intentions may be genuine, I've learnt over the years through Mike Murdock that *'wisdom is not only knowing what to say but knowing when to say it and how to say it'.* There's just got to be focal point that balances the whole equation out.

I believe it's one thing to speak of love, it's another thing to act it out. I've seen couples with just girls and couples with just boys perfectly enjoying the whole journey of parenthood. Time is so precious, if you constantly worry or complain over things that you cannot control while refusing to see or celebrate the precious gifts you've been given then, you are simply trashing the gift of time.

Like I've earlier said, the journey is as important as the destination. Celebrate the beautiful humans you've been blessed with irrespective of your anticipated gender. This is my personal opinion and advice.

However, if you feel you've been guilty of such acts in the past, today is just the best time to turn a new leaf and set things straight. Let go of your fears and shed the weight imposed on you by societal beliefs because the only thing worse than being physically imprisoned is mental and emotional imprisonment.

While Physical imprisonment and abuse leaves victims with external bruises of all sorts with tangible aches that will probably linger for a while, Mental and Emotional imprisonment leaves victims with psychological scars that might linger for more than a while. The torture is personal and almost infinite if the victim does not go out of his/her way to shout for help. This is why it's important to know what is best for you and go for it because if you wait for others to decipher your pain, you might wait forever as their minds are pre-occupied with lots of other important things. Learn to travel light on this flight called life by leaving what's beyond your control to God. Take a cue from the serenity prayer:

"Grant me the serenity to accept the things I cannot change, the courage to change the things I can and the wisdom to know the difference."

– Reinhold Niebuhr

Chapter Seven

Waiting for the C-tuation to Fade Away

As I write this particular chapter, we're few days' shy of Easter in 2020. What's the importance of bringing that up right here? That's because earlier on this year, precisely in January I began writing this book with a clear-cut direction inspired by Trinity and the level of pain and impatience I saw people experience in the various phases on their lives journey. No matter how much they tried to hide it, it was raising its head whenever we spoke. I'd like to call it a subtle shadow that loved *peek-a-boo*.

Unfortunately, the plague of Covid-19 also came heavy on a global scale. To know that I began writing this book without any knowledge that anything of the sort which was heavy enough to place a global weight of waiting humbled me even more. Truly, we all claimed to have no time until all we had left right now is time.

Once again, the uncertainties crept in. Rumors flying through every entry point of social media, fears sky-rocketing, people's job in the middle of the road, boredom on a new high, believer's trembling, politicians embezzling, youths making a global difference with interesting social challenges for fun, war-front filled with PPEs(Personal Protective Equipments) over bombs and every possible business leveraging the internet.

Just like Isaac Oyedepo said, even if you were not infected with the virus chances are you were definitely being affected in a way. The lockdown was sufficient to alter your routine and if you had kids (especially the little ones), be sure of the fact that more than ever your appreciation of teachers just went through the roof.

Not sure if by the time this book gets to your hand the pandemic will still be on or not. We really pray it'd be behind us in no time. Nevertheless, there's always a message in every mess. This C-tuation has simply shown us what is important. For instance, if you thought all those things that got you worried, agitated and angry at as stated in the previous chapters were that important, this C-tuation must have taken the weight off that and though it might have brought a new weight of waiting upon us but in all it definitely placed things in perspective. The importance of majoring on major things and not minor things has definitely taken root.

Currently, people value their jobs more (even the jobs they once hated), friends more, families more, most importantly they value even the breath of fresh air much more and the introverts value the blessing of social gatherings way more than ever. All the worries prior to Covid-19 has automatically been gone with the wind because you just can't find anyone at this present moment getting saddened over certain things. The only thing that is checked on a daily basis to ensure its intact is good health with the believe that once there is life, there's hope. It should actually be a moment in which we all get to ponder on the most important things and if you're still not clear about what that will look like in your world.

Here's a poem to help you see clearer:

If you want to know the value of one year, just ask a student who failed a course.

If you want to know the value of one month, ask a mother who gave birth to a premature baby.

If you want to know the value of one hour, ask the lovers waiting to meet.

If you want to know the value of one minute, ask the person who just missed the bus.

If you want to know the value of one second, ask the person who just escaped death in a car accident.

If you want to know the value of one-hundredth of a second, ask the athlete who won a silver medal in the Olympics.

-Marc Levy

Chapter Eight

Silencing the Negative Voices in your Life

The bus-stop we've waited for has finally arrived, the place you get to eventually own your voice and silence the negative voices in your life. At this point, you can give yourself a pat at the back to say yes, I made it against all odds!!!

Ever heard of that saying *'laugh at yourself first and others will be late if they ever have to'*. The very first thing you need to know is you've got to face the facts. Own your story. Be true to you. Upon this bedrock of reality, your foundation becomes unshakable.

Pause for a minute right here and do this exercise: Think about that very thing you think people have laughed at you for, whether in the past or presently. How did it make you feel? What fears grew as a result of that even when you tried to ignore it?

Back to reality – which is reading this chapter – the only reason that situation or person made you feel that way is because you permitted them. You signed the consent letter. You allowed that to happen.

A while ago I discovered this truth "whenever you fail to accept the totality of who you truly are (good and bad), you unconsciously give others the permission to become the author of your life. So they begin to feel like they hold the mic to sing your song even better. Remember, they are not to blame when this happens. You are! Because somewhere deep down, there's still a part of you that you failed to fully accept you.

Read an inspiring story of a man called John Foppe, born without arms. While he was young he was laughed at all through, at different phases in his life he literally wished he wasn't born yet his parents never gave up on reminding him of how much of a genius he was. Then, one day he came to himself and accepted himself (accepted his disabilities, accepted his 'YOUniqueness' and everything that came with it) from that day, his life took a brand new turn.

In case you're thinking your story is far from this, have you ever been a drop-out of school. Not once but twice. The very first time you were expelled from school, the next school you got into, you dropped out. Do you know what that means as the first son in an African–Nigerian family? I had to include the location for emphasis so you know what it means. This right there was Steve Harris' story. He felt worthless until the time that he began to fully accept himself and even laugh at himself while making a difference in the lives of people. He's gone on to become one of the top coaches with a nickname of Ruthless Executioner.

Guess what? The fact that he used his failure story to inspire the world readily makes any other person trying to use his story to sabotage him look stupid! That's the magic of owning your story and staying true.

Sometimes, the weight of waiting happens in the relationship circle whether it's a single looking for the perfect one or married couple trusting God for their baby. I fully understand what that feels like yet you need to truly define what really makes the wait seem so weighty. If you're one of those thinking this will feel a lot better if I travel out of the country probably because at least the constant prying on you by family and friends will ease off a bit. #SpoilerAlert. Distance is usually not that much of a barrier when it comes to things like that or didn't they say blood is thicker than water. You really can't run from yourself which is why you need to learn to accept yourself.

Rather than trying to escape crucial conversations, sometimes there's a need to face it. Depending on the situation any of this strategies can be applied:

GIVE A LISTENING EAR AND A BLANK CANVAS

This is like giving the person a blank canvas to design their thoughts about you. Listen to them using an open heart irrespective of your perception of the person. Sometimes perception can be based on assumption and not factual. Giving people benefit of doubt helps in two ways. First, you listen with an open heart simply seeing (or trusting for) the best in them. Next, it helps to keep your heart at peace. The state of your heart is important for you. Life is a journey of a thousand or more like a zillion miles and travelling light (not just physically but emotionally and mentally) is important for you especially if you want to go far. So it really is okay to give people benefit of doubt and hear what they've got to say.

WHAT DID THE CANVAS REVEAL?

After giving them a listening ear and a blank canvas, understand that everyone in your world can be placed as either a Confidant, a Constituent or a Comrade. You've got to figure out who they really are.

A *Confidant* is for you come rain or shine, he/she will stick with you when the going gets tough. If you've got 5 in your lifetime you're a blessed person.

A *Constituent* is only for what you are for. They probably have the same values with you and will stand by you whenever it's time to prove that you both are on the same page. They are not solely for you. They are for what you are for. There's a common belief that bonds you both.

A *Comrade* is against what you are against. A Comrade is not for you but is against what you are against. If you both have a common person you dislike, then you both will look like friends only for that season.

It is dangerous to mistake one of the C's for another. The damage it can cause you might be costly. Hence, it's important to know where each person in your world really stands.

TIME TO SPEAK UP

No one is a mind-reader, most people that claim to be one usually end up riding the waves of assumption which is dangerous. If you don't tell people who you are, they will assume who you are not. Your voice has power. Oh wow! Look at your mates getting married, when are you settling down? Is there a problem with your wife/husband because I'm expecting my grandchild? How come you haven't gotten a job yet? Are you guys going to try again for a boy? Is it this course that will fetch you a great future? That your business, won't you put it aside and look for a job?

I've seen people chicken out of questions because they feel broken or better still they want to be in people's good-books. I was once there so I truly can understand but here's what I learnt. When people speak to you, you get hurt and then you even discover that words can pierce to the soul right? They go around feeling fly because in their minds – they've won! You made them win! They had the final say, final words, final laugh. Guess what gave them wings? It wasn't because they said something so hurtful. Nah. It was your loud silence that gave them the jackpot.

Here's how you flip the script, when people ask questions or make statements that you sense are not just because they care per se but to ridicule you in a way, be present in listening to their question. You can gain access to a person's motive just by listening intentionally and observing their non-verbal expressions. Once you discern that, you can sometimes answer their question by putting them in your shoes and throwing the question back at them (*just in case you run out of ideas*). For instance, you could respond by saying, if you were in this position right now, how would you handle it? This method works. It simply seeks to know if they've got a solution for you and if they truly care. This way your question is more than a slingshot that checks for answers because it also detects their true intentions.

Listen up guys/ladies, if you're reading this book, you're grown enough to know that your voice counts.

CHECK THE FORECAST OF THEIR LIFESTYLE

As we progress in life, we realize that what used to matter so much at a point in our lives, doesn't anymore. I know my last point said you should speak up but I'm sure you've also heard how wise it is to *choose your battles*. Growing up I just felt so terribly burdened with pain whenever someone pointed something they felt will ruin me. It could be the fact that I was too quiet for them when they felt I should be outspoken and I would blame myself for my personality.

Until I grew wiser and got to know that everyone is wired differently. So whenever those same people tried attacking my personality and uniqueness later on (if they happened to be people that would never lose an argument because such environment made them flourish), I would safeguard my peace and gladly relax on the sofa of awareness. Awareness that they probably have no idea about the fact that there are different personalities that exist and I can never be them and vice versa. In that case, rather than feel burdened and saddened, I end up feeling really sorry for them because obviously had they known better, they'd have done better.

There's a possibility that due to one's upbringing, some people might see a C-section as forbidden or flawed in some parts of the world. In some cases, especially in the religious minds, there's a tendency of seeing the woman to be less of a Hebrew woman. Yet, the question I have is will you desire to spend your precious time explaining over and again to people who have chosen to judge you rather than inquire about your reason behind your choice? Your guess is as good as mine.

In retrospect, I'd say some people are not as enlightened as others, few years ago I was probably at the other end of the line with a linear mindset of just one possible means by which pregnant women could give birth but during my pregnancy I was equipped with information as I read a lot and had an open mind and as I read, I was sure to carry my husband along as well on some interesting discoveries. That gentle nudge of different sides to pregnancy and delivery really came in handy for us. So much that afterwards we realized that just the privilege of birthing a baby irrespective of how that baby is birthed and being able to come out alive (mother and child) is purely a miracle that should be celebrated.

There are couples blessed with two beautiful girls or boys and deep down they are satisfied but the voices in their heads keep placing them on the hot seat, do not let what people think you should do or shouldn't do become the compass of your life.

WHERE ARE THEY SPEAKING FROM???

Is it a place of fear? Most of our parents got married when they were 16-22years. A dear friend of mine says all our parents are in the same WhatsApp group especially when it comes to their thinking patterns. You might argue that out but keep in mind the *context*. Most people speak from personal experiences, very few speak from a place of inspiration or revelation. Herein lies the difference.

KNOW WHAT TO TAKE AND WHAT TO TRASH

Although this point has been stated above, it needs to be reiterated that anyone that puts so much fear into you (whether in relation to marriage, job, lifestyle, business, pandemic etc.) and does not offer a solution of how to overcome that fear. It's important you trash such information.

Chapter Nine

The Wait is Over!

By now, without a doubt in mind you've mastered how to shed the weight of your wait but there's just one more thing. I really need you to understand that even though the wait might not be easy, as you embrace your journey and own your story you'd discover that in the end it will all be worth it.

Can you imagine running a race looking sideways or backwards? It won't be long before you might get left behind as distractions often leads to disappointment. You need to harness the power of focus.

There is a story of a Chinese farmer whose horse ran away and all the neighbours came around that evening and said "*that's too bad*" and he said "*maybe*". The next day the horse came back and brought with it 7 wild horses and all the neighbours came back and said "*Wow, that's great! Isn't it*" and he said "*maybe*". On a certain day, his son was attempting to tame one of these horses while riding it and was thrown off of it and broke his leg and all the neighbours came around and said *"Well, that's too bad! Isn't it"* and the farmer said *"maybe"*. The next day, the conscription officers came around looking for young men to join the army and they rejected his son because he had a broken leg. The neighbours came around in the evening and said *"Isn't that Wonderful"* and the farmer said *"maybe"*.

The whole process of nature and life is an integrated process; it is easy to give up or get frustrated when looking at the glass half-empty but you can upgrade your perspective by understanding that everything happening to you is actually happening for you. The Chinese farmer's perspective made him unmovable even in the face of calamity and this is how we are supposed to live.

Staying focused is the ultimate way to a healthier, wealthier and happier journey. Just like a software subsequently releases new versions for updates, your human software should be wired in a way that minimum every 6months there should be a new release of a higher version of yourself. This should be your goal. It would have been more appropriate to make it quarterly or even daily but since everyone is not on the same level, I'd say every 6 months.

Some things take time, the gestation period of a chicken and that of an elephant is not the same. This is not to say you should twist this statement by giving yourself flimsy excuses but be realistic and true to yourself. Let your number one competition remain the person you see in the mirror.

I wish you the very best in this beautiful journey called life as you aim to travel light, may your experience remain wholesome.

I'm excitedly waiting to hear how this book helped you to shed some weight of waiting or answer some burning questions in your heart. I'd love to hear your story. You can send a DM on Instagram/Twitter/Facebook – @peacecodybanks , email via pz.codybanks@gmail.com or feel free to visit my website and subscribe to my newsletters at www.themindofcodybanks.com.

About the Author

Peace Amienghemhen (popularly known as CodyBanks) is a Dream Activator and Coach on a mission to identify and activate the hidden treasures in youths by helping them gain clarity and accelerated momentum on their journey.

She is the founder of CodyBanks Mentoring Academy (www.themindofcodybanks.com) and Unplugged Bootcamp. Both platforms equip people with laser-focused trainings geared towards activating their hidden treasures.

As a Digital Strategist, she holds a Masters in Information Systems Management from University of Salford, Manchester and constantly seeks to proffer digital solutions to individuals and corporations.

Peace is happily married to Ben and they are blessed with a son.

www.ingramcontent.com/pod-product-compliance
Lightning Source LLC
Chambersburg PA
CBHW032110091125
35189CB00033B/460